All About Animals

Elephants

By Sarah Albee

Reader's Digest Young Families

Contents

Chapter 1
An Elephant Story

Little Elephant looked up. Dark clouds were zooming across the sky. The long, dry season was coming to an end at last. Her mother stood nearby, along with several of Little Elephant's aunts, all of them keeping a close eye on their little ones.

Every day Little Elephant was able to do more for herself. Soon her mother would be ready to have another baby. Little Elephant couldn't wait to have a new brother or sister to play with!

The elephants in the herd stomped and snorted restlessly. Big drops of rain began to fall. Little Elephant's skin shone as she grew wetter. The rain felt wonderful!

For the next week or so, the herd trudged across the wide-open plains. Now that the rainy season had arrived, the elephants were following Big Elephant to the river. She was the largest elephant in the herd and had lived a very long time. She knew just where to go. And she was Little Elephant's great-aunt!

Is it true that elephants never forget?

Elephants have very large brains and good memories. Older elephants remember paths that lead to good feeding areas and water holes. They often recognize distant relatives.

7

Little Elephant's group arrived at the marshlands near the river, where tender green reeds grew quickly. There was plenty of food and water for everyone. Little Elephant trumpeted happily. She had spotted another group of elephants! They were part of a larger clan that shared a home range with Little Elephant's group.

It was not a coincidence that the groups had joined up. Big Elephant had been sending signals to the other group as they crossed the grassy plain, low rumbles that no human could ever hear. The other elephants had signaled back, telling Big Elephant just where they were.

Little Elephant hurried over to greet the young elephants in the group. They twined their trunks around one another, trotted in circles, roared, and rumbled. Then Little Elephant and her friends jumped into the muddy water and rolled and splashed. They picked up gobs of mud with their trunks and slapped it against their bodies to cool off.

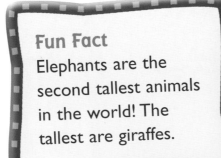

Fun Fact
Elephants are the second tallest animals in the world! The tallest are giraffes.

Suddenly Big Elephant let out a bellow. All the elephants started to stomp and snort and trumpet with joy. A new baby boy elephant had been born to Little Elephant's mother!

When Big Elephant gave the signal, Little Elephant hurried over to greet her new baby brother. Using her tusks and her trunk, their mother was gently helping him to stand up on his wobbly legs. He was learning to balance himself on his four legs. Little Elephant touched him gently with her trunk. She had so much to teach her little brother about being an elephant!

Furry Babies

Baby elephants are born with black fur covering their skin. Most of it falls off. When baby elephants grow up, they will continue to have thick hairs at the end of their tails and a little hair on their faces.

Like lions, bears, rabbits, and humans, elephants belong to the group of animals scientists call mammals. And all mammals have hair.

Chapter 2

The Body of an Elephant

The huge ears of African elephants are the same shape as the continent of Africa!

The Biggest
Elephants are the largest land animals in the world.

Two Kinds of Elephants

There are two kinds of elephants. One lives in Asia. The other lives in Africa. The biggest difference between the two is the size of their ears. Asian elephants have much smaller, pointier ears. African elephants have enormous ears that are rounder in shape and rise above their necks.

Asian elephants are shorter and smaller than their African relatives. Asian elephants are about 9 feet tall at the shoulder compared with African elephants, which are 10 to 13 feet tall.

Asian elephants are somewhat different in shape, too. They have more of a dome-shaped head and a rounder body with a humped back. The backs of African elephants have a slight dip in the middle.

All African elephants have tusks. The tusks are very big. In Asia, only male elephants have tusks.

The trunks of African elephants have two "fingers" at the tip. Asian elephants have only one.

Asian Elephants

Asian elephants are smaller than African elephants and have smaller ears. They have two bumps on their foreheads.

Fingertips!

An African elephant's trunk has two flexible flaps at the tip that work together, somewhat like your thumb and pointer finger, to pick up small objects. In Asia, an elephant's trunk has just one flap, and it also works like a finger.

The trunk of an elephant serves as the animal's hand and nose. It can do many amazing things.

A Hunk of a Trunk

The trunk of an elephant is awesome! It is strong enough to lift a 600-pound log and dainty enough to pluck a single blade of grass. It can bend, twist, stretch, and curl. It can suck up, spray, or hold over two gallons of water. It is loaded with taste and smell sensors—elephants can smell water miles away. The trunk caresses other elephants, maybe to show affection and tenderness. The main task of a trunk, though, is to carry food and water to the elephant's mouth.

The trunk is a continuation of the elephant's nose and upper lip. It can be as long as 6 feet and has no bones in it at all. It is made completely of muscle—some scientists think it has more than 40,000 separate muscles!

What's Up?

Elephants use their trunks to touch or rub one another to say hello. They may also twist their trunks together, somewhat like us shaking hands!

Giant-Size Teeth

An elephant's tusks are just as awesome as its trunk! Tusks are giant-size incisor teeth, and they continue to grow throughout the animal's lifetime. The tusks of a male elephant can be more than 10 feet long! Tusks are used for digging, peeling bark from trees, lifting things, and when necessary, as weapons. In Africa all elephants grow tusks. Among Asian elephants, only males develop tusks.

In addition to tusks, elephants have four huge teeth inside their mouths. One tooth can weigh more than 11 pounds! Like your molars, elephant teeth have ridges for grinding up food. When a tooth gets worn out, a new one grows in. Elephants grow six sets of teeth in their lifetime! The last set grows in about the time that the animal turns 40 years old!

Ivory Tusks

Unfortunately for elephants, humans have prized ivory over the centuries. Because elephants are now an endangered species, the business of selling ivory has been banned. Still, illegal ivory hunters exist.

Elephants use one tusk more than the other, just as we use one hand more than the other. The main tusk is rounder at the tip from use and sometimes shorter than the other tusk.

On Tiptoe

Elephants are very sure-footed. They step quickly and almost soundlessly, which is surprising in such large animals!

Elephants have toes, although we can only see some of the toenails. Elephants walk by putting their toes down first, then the heel. The elephant's weight is supported both by the tip of the toe and a thick, squishy foot pad in the heel that acts as a cushion.

The foot pad is actually a spongy layer of skin that expands as the foot is placed down. The ridges on the bottoms of an elephant's feet grip the ground much the way a person's hiking boots do, allowing the elephant to climb hills and walk on rocks quite easily.

Elephants can support their weight on their hind legs. This enables them to reach leaves that grow high on trees.

Elephants can walk forward and backward. They can run and swim, but they cannot jump.

On the Go

Elephants walk several miles in a day and may travel as many as fifty. They usually move at about four to five miles an hour, but they can sprint (for a short distance) at a rate of 30 miles per hour. That's faster than the fastest human marathon runners, who run only 13 miles per hour!

The skin of elephants is very thick, but it is also very sensitive. An elephant can feel a fly landing on its skin!

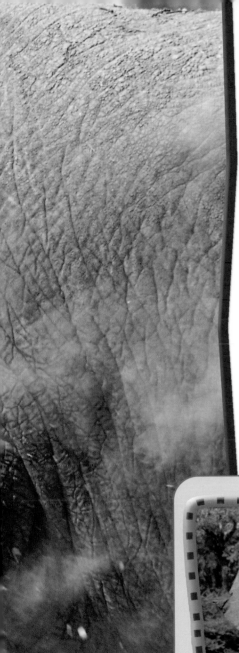

Wrinkly Skin

Elephant skin is very wrinkly. African elephants have wrinklier skin than their Asian relatives. The wrinkles come in handy. They allow the animal to move about freely, as if dressed in a roomy suit of clothes, to bend and kneel and run. Also, the cracks and grooves in the skin trap water and mud, allowing slow evaporation of water. This helps keep the elephant cool on hot days. The mud helps prevent sunburn, too.

Another word for an elephant is a pachyderm (pronounced *PACK-ih-derm*). It is the Greek word for "thick-skinned." The skin of an elephant can be as much as $1\frac{1}{2}$ inches thick in some places. But although it is thick, an elephant's skin is very sensitive.

"Ear" Conditioning

Elephant ears are perfect natural air conditioners. The ears have lots of blood vessels close to the surface of the skin. As air moves over the ears, it cools the blood vessels. Cooler blood then circulates around the elephant's body.

African elephant ears can wave like huge fans, letting body heat escape.

Chapter 3
Meals and Baths

Elephants can spend 16 hours a day eating!

Elephant Aid
If an elephant is sick and can't walk to food, other members of the family will bring food to her.

What Elephants Eat

Elephants need to eat enormous amounts of food to support their huge size. A large male can eat more than 500 pounds of food every day! This explains why elephants spend most of their day eating. Elephants are herbivores, which means they eat only plant matter and no meat. In addition to grasses, leaves, and fruits, elephants eat twigs and tree bark.

Like other herbivores, elephants crave salt and other minerals that plants do not provide. So elephants eat the soil, because it has the nutrients they need. Like natural bulldozers, elephants dig up the earth with their tusks, grind the soil and rock into powder with their teeth, and swallow.

Hungry elephants in search of food can be very destructive, especially when food is scarce. Elephants will strip shrubs of leaves and knock down trees to get at the leaves on top. But elephants change the landscape in good ways, too. By eating shrubs and small trees, they thin out thickly wooded areas, letting in sunshine for new plants to grow. And since elephants don't fully digest all that they eat, their dung contains seeds that help to spread new plant life.

Three Meals a Day

Although elephants spend most of their time eating, they eat three "meals" a day just like you — morning, afternoon, and night.

At noon, when the sun is hottest, elephants find shade and sometimes doze while standing up.
At night, though, they lie down on their side to sleep.

Water Wonders

Water is very important to elephants, and they never go very far from it. Elephants need to drink a lot of water to survive. Just one elephant can drink more than 40 gallons of water a day! To drink, an elephant draws up water with its trunk and then squirts the water into its mouth. A baby elephant has to kneel down to drink until it learns how to use its trunk.

Elephants love to soak in watering holes. Soaking in deep water lets the elephant take weight off its feet and legs, something which must come as a great relief for an animal that can weigh 7 tons!

Elephants also love to swim. They can swim several miles at one time. They may even use their trunks as snorkels.

Sometimes, during periods of drought, water may not be visible, but older elephants are very good at finding it. They loosen the soil with their tusks and use their trunks to dig. And they can dig holes that are more than 6 feet deep! Other animals know that elephants can find hidden water, and so they often follow elephants, hoping to benefit from their natural well-digging services.

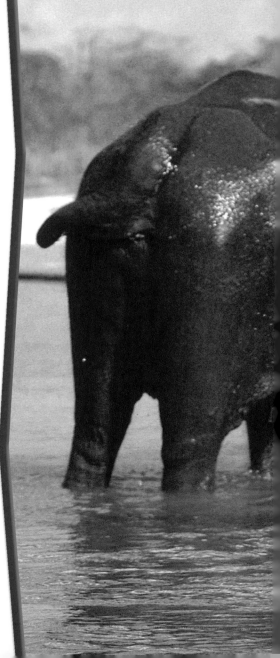

Elephants love to play in the water. They splash and spray for fun as well as to cool down and to get rid of pesky insects.

Mud Baths

After bathing, elephants dust themselves with dirt or roll in the mud to coat themselves. The mud keeps the animals cool and their skin soft. It also helps protect against insects and sunburn. Covered in mud, young elephants have fun slipping and sliding over each other. Sometimes older elephants join in and play!

Chapter 4
Elephant Families

Elephants are very caring animals. If a baby elephant takes a nap, the group will wait until it awakens before moving on. If a member of the herd is sick or wounded, the other elephants will not leave it.

Keeping in Touch

Elephants live in small family groups of about 8 to 10 animals. The group is led by a female elephant. Scientists call her the matriarch (pronounced *MAY-tree-ark*). She is usually the oldest animal in the group, often more than 60 years old, and the elephant with the most experience. Since elephants continue to grow throughout their lives, the matriarch is also the herd's largest animal. The matriarch is responsible for the safety of the group and making sure all the elephants have enough food and water. When groups of elephants travel or stay together for a time, they are called a herd of elephants.

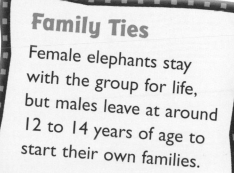

Family Ties

Female elephants stay with the group for life, but males leave at around 12 to 14 years of age to start their own families.

Elephants keep in contact with each other by sounds. Their usual call is a low rumbling noise. Humans cannot hear it, but other elephants can — even if they are six miles away! Other sounds elephants make are trumpet calls, roars, and screams.

Like people, elephants communicate using body language. When they are relaxed, their trunks hang down, and their ears are back. When they are angry, they flare out their ears, pull back their trunks, and tuck their heads down with their tusks pointing forward. Elephants warn away intruders by making threatening signals, such as whirling their trunks around, beating them against the ground, or tossing up a cloud of dust.

Big Babies

When a mother elephant is ready to have a baby, the other elephants in the group gather around to protect her from any predators. One female helps her with the birth. The newborn elephant, called a calf, weighs more than 200 pounds and is about 3 feet tall! Within an hour, the calf can stand up on its own. All the elephants welcome the big little one by stomping their feet and making trumpet calls.

The mother elephant is very protective of her baby and rarely lets it out of her sight. For the first few months, the baby elephant lives only on its mother's milk, then adds plant food to its diet. A calf will drink about 7 gallons of milk a day until age two. By six years of age, Asian elephants can weigh a ton, or 2,000 pounds! Because they drink mother's milk, young elephants can spend a lot of time playing rather than having to search for food. Playing helps them learn important skills for survival. Calves run around, charge after birds, and play-fight.

Like humans, elephants have a long childhood. They learn many skills from the older elephants in their group. Sisters, aunts, and grandmothers help the mothers take care of and teach the young elephants.

A Comfort Trunk

An elephant calf sucks on its trunk for comfort just as a human baby does with his thumb!

One at a Time

Female elephants give birth to just one baby elephant at a time. Scientists call the baby a calf. Female elephants may have four to six calves during their lifetime.

A baby elephant is small enough to walk under its mother's belly, where it will be very safe. A young calf often wraps its trunk around the mother's tail so the pair won't get separated from each other.

Chapter 5
Past and Future

Hyraxes, like this furry fellow, don't look anything at all like elephants, but scientists say they (and manatees) are the closest living relatives of elephants today!

Big and Small Relatives

The ancient relatives of elephants belong to a group of animals scientists call *Proboscidea* ("animals with a trunk"). Mammoths and mastodons, which became extinct about 10,000 years ago, were members of this group. They were nearly the same size as modern-day elephants but had long, shaggy fur and huge, curled, 16-foot-long tusks. Woolly mammoths lived in very cold places.

The closest living relatives of elephants today include hyraxes (furry, rabbit-size mammals) and manatees (sea cows). Hyraxes don't look anything like elephants, but they have a few things in common with them — an ancient ancestor, toenails, cushioned foot pads, two extra-large front teeth, and the shapes of some bones. Long ago, hyraxes were the size of oxen. Hyraxes live in Africa and some parts of the Middle East.

Fast Facts About Elephants

Scientific name	African elephant	*Loxodonta africana*
	Asian elephant	*Elephas maximus*
Class	Mammals	
Order	Proboscidea (animals with trunks)	
Size	African elephant (male) 10-13 feet tall	
	Asian elephant (male) 9 feet tall	
Weight	African elephant (male) 6 tons	
	Asian elephant (male) 5 tons	
Life span	Up to 80 years	
Habitat	African elephant	savanna, forest
	Asian elephant	forest, grassland

You Can Help!

You help save elephants from extinction every time you reuse or recycle paper, metal, and glass. Your effort helps to slow the rate at which elephant habitats are disappearing.

Elephants live in a wide range of habitats, from savannas to forests. When the sun is hottest, they seek whatever shade they can find.

Where Elephants Live

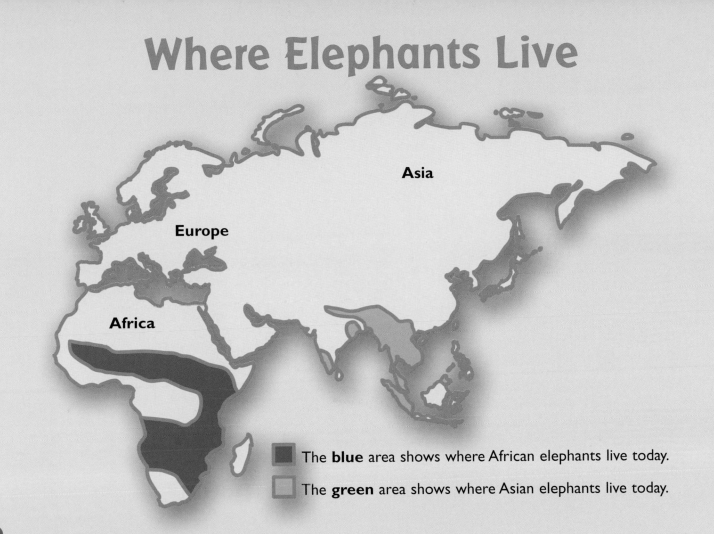

Asia

Europe

Africa

The **blue** area shows where African elephants live today.

The **green** area shows where Asian elephants live today.

Because of their huge size, elephants have little to fear from predators. Although baby elephants may be hunted by lions (in Africa) or tigers (in Asia), they are usually well protected by adult elephants in the group.

The single greatest threat to elephants is humans. Elephant tusks are made of ivory, which has been highly prized for centuries. To take an elephant's tusks, the elephant must be killed first. Although the trading of ivory was banned in 1989, ivory continues to be sold illegally and elephants continue to be killed.

Another big cause of the decline in the number of elephants is the destruction of their habitats. Elephants once lived throughout Africa, but now live in just one-third of the continent. Land in Asia and Africa continues to be cleared for farming, lumber, mining, and buildings for humans.

Glossary of Wild Words

banned   forbidden by law

calf   a young elephant

drought   a period of time during which there is little or no rain

habitat   the natural environment where an animal or plant lives

herbivore   an animal that eats only plants

incisor   a kind of tooth. An elephant's tusks are very, very long incisors

ivory   a smooth, hard white substance that forms the tusks of elephants and other animals

mammal   an animal with a backbone and hair on its body that drinks milk from its mother when it is born

matriarch   female leader of a group

pachyderm   another word for elephant. It comes from the Greek word for "thick-skinned."

Are elephants smart?

Elephants communicate with one another and pass information from one generation to the next. They take care of each other. They use tools. For example, they pick up sticks with their trunks to scratch itches they can't reach. They plan, such as when they dig holes for water, drink, cover the holes up with soil and branches, and return at a later time to drink again. They can learn tricks and remember them for a long time—some say forever.

predator	an animal that hunts and eats other animals to survive
proboscidea	ancient relatives of elephants that included mastodons and mammoths
savanna	a flat grassland area with scattered trees in a hot region of the world
sea cow	a modern relative of the elephant that lives in the ocean. Also called a manatee.
species	a group of plants or animals that are the same in many ways
trunk	the long, flexible snout of an elephant
tusk	a very long, pointed tooth that sticks far out from the side of an animal's mouth, usually one of a pair
visible	able to be seen

Index